In The Islands of Chile, *David Nash off[...]*
world through poetry whose aim is 'not to [...]
into yourself.'

Nash riffs on the variousness of Chile's islar[...]
self, world and other, as we labour under th[...]

This is ecologically minded work, exquisitely ιuned to the world's conditional
fragility and ablaze with its own truths and a fierce eros in which 'to be touched / is
to be proven.'

Always aware of the fallibilities and slippage of language where 'you are not quite your
name' these poems are singular, tender and often breathtaking. Nash wrests with the
stuff of language, and lets the reader in on the act, seeking lived truths, stalking love,
capturing the strangeness and beauty of sentience.

The Islands of Chile *is a dazzling, curious and indefinably brilliant debut. Read it and*
come alive.

Sarah Westcott

Using a variety of experimental approaches and with a singular originality, David Nash
constructs a compelling debut publication that grows in power through each section.

Place, the naming of place and the author's relationship with it, the natural world,
addresses to loved ones and a consideration of the self, all are seamlessly braided together,
occasionally seasoned by an awareness of broader culture and more demotic notes. The
undercurrent throughout is queer love, presented here with original flair, the eroticism
often surfacing from surprising angles.

The narrative arc develops and grows in intensity, culminating in a final section
powerfully focused on mortality and presented in prose form. It is as if the poetry itself
has broken into islands, an effect lightly presaged in the prologue which is a slender poem
with barely any lines or words.

Nash doesn't merely inhabit the islands of Chile; they inhabit him. This pamphlet is
more than 'promising', conveying the accomplishment of a first book. More please.

Eva Salzman

First published in 2022 by Fourteen Publishing.
fourteenpoems.com

Design and typeset by Stromberg Design.
strombergdesign.co.uk

Proofreading and copy editing by Lara Kavanagh.
lk-copy.com

Printed by Print2Demand Ltd, Westoning, Bedfordshire, UK.

ISBN:
978-1-8383943-8-7

The Islands of Chile

David Nash

I like maps because they lie
Because they give no access to the vicious truth.
Because good-heartedly, good-naturedly
They spread before me a world
Not of this world
                    —*from* Map, *Wisława Szymborska*

because of Ignacio

contents:

I
as in
me,
the
least
fussy
of shapes,
the femur
which
articulates
the thigh.
One line
waiting
to be
qualified:
by a
verb,
by a
full
stop,
by an
ellipsis,
but
even so,
anyway,
alone.
Undressed,
a wire
with a
message
at both
ends.
The
grasped
ba nn
i   st
e   r,
in   a
    uni
ver se
of cur
ves. The
primary
number,
the p
alindr
o me -
o ne
f rom
e very
di rec
t ion.
O ne
   f or every
   p air of
     eyes. One

simple
stroke of
the han d.

I

Isla Grande de Chiloé / Ireland

42°40'36 S, 73°59'36 W / 53°25 N, 8°0 S

We're the same.
Your hands have known more work and your teeth are whiter
but we're the same.
Only in the rear-view mirror does your form shift,
like mine does.
When your rivers are cold they do not know they are cold.
My rivers, too, are simple things.
You have made compromises to beauty; I am less beautiful than I could be.
We're the same.
You can turn the rain and you have a heartbeat that you take for granted.
So do I.
You are not quite your name.
We're the same.
What have you cast off in translation? What have you won?
What have I?
You are surrounded. You are greener and less green. Your scent is yours alone.
We're the same.
Look, how your waters end up in mine.

Isla Falsa   (False Island)

43.59'43°S, 72.99'98°W

There are no small parts.
I take what light I can.
If they want farce, I'll do myself up and
I'll wear my pearls, I'll be all fuss and chewed nails.
Then there's comedy: comedy is all the seasons in one day,
and cleavage marked in rings of altitude.
Have you seen me slumped in white garments
and wringing my hands, dropping fruit? That's tragedy.
I do not need an audience – the act is reward enough.
The sun is a rose flung upwards.
The rainfall sounds so much like applause.

Isla Ascención   (Ascension Island)

43°52'20 S / 73°47'59 W

It happened that the island just went up.
It had done its duty. It had lain still and been something
for the sea to molest. It had taken flagpole after flagpole,
had flourished or rotted according to the season.
In short, it can't be said to have not been an island.

Some Deus-ex-machina magpie, prizing a glint
it had spied in the island, finds purchase in it,
mounts the wind, and lifts the whole thing up.
Up like a communion wafer, up like a tablet of stone,
up like Mary, her purpose birthed.

The island sighs into cloud,
watches from above its own absence.

Islotes de los Amigos   (Isles of Friends, or Our Word)

43.61'32°S, 72.95'75°W

We don't believe in love, and so
don't love.
We are calling time on endlessness, guff,

commotion, and deeds. Nature is dead.
The coupled yew trees are dead.
So too high tides, and swellings of the ocean set to music.

We've had enough of these words: epic,
bones, soil, depths, rust, dust, desperately.
From now on, the limp water-puckers of the city's

river will do as waves,
and we will build warm piping to stay
the impetuous snow. We want

a lace-knit fog, and
to worship a rain
that can't quite rain,

muck that apologises for mucking.
We'll put a vulture out among
the swans and minus them

of their pretensions. We'll come
in like men of law, red-taping the sun to within
inches, deflating crescendoes, putting taxes on the smell of skin.

Look, we want to speak a word that cannot bear to be defined,
much less interpreted, the kind
of word that shuns the crutch-scaffolding

of speakers and can't be held, does all the holding.

Listen, says our word. *I am*
the truest version of you. Do you understand? I am.

We are.

Isla Inútil   (Useless Island)

55.1'29 S, 68.14'44 W

is what they landed on, eventually. because i am:

just a close-up of a bus seat cover

today's dust, in the way it happens to have fallen

when a cat yawns – the shape and shade of that, more or less

the chalkmark outline of an immigrant

remember flakes of limescale, before you started using water filters? those

the most used letter on the keyboard

a child's glove you saw on the way to somewhere

logos of small enterprises

i could go on. but you there,

you don't need to see more. you see so much already

Isla Darwin

54.55'51°S, 70.8'36°W

is an oil lamp
tipped on its side
and as such it has two
defining characteristics:
euphoria and anguish, the
puma sated and the puma starved
its back muscles making their hundred
faces as though reflected on the back of
a spoon, as bright and as dumb as metal,
bright and dumb in the same way that an
avocado doesn't know itself to be an avocado
neither if it has fallen nor if it has further yet to
fall; as bright and as dumb as the meatus, which
has seen things you could never have seen, and winks,
a little wound on the horizon that promises to heal and
doesn't and then promises to bleed, but goes as dry as a
sand dune, one of those dunes that you think of when you
hear the word 'desert': fine, luxurious even, but not desirable,
because you know, don't you, that deserts are not like that in real
life, and oases are common as muck – they're just islands, oil lamps,
pumas, muscles, faces, spoons, metals, avocados, that little slit at the
top of a penis, a wink, a wound, a sand dune, a desert, an oasis, an island.

Isla Verde I   (Green Island, or Taking)

31°86'54 S, 71°53'86 W

I took to the tree by giving, first by climbing
since that is how height is earned, and that is how I'd learned if things
could bear me. It could, and I went higher, and the sap quickened.
Deeper now, and having seen the seasons from its prow, could put my hand
with certainty on where best to tap for glue or crack off an arrow.
I knew the route that the water took, root to leaf-tip, as though you
were the deer and I the deer's blood, steering from hoof to heart and into the
antler.
A good start: to try the bark and find the bark worth trying, and worth
trying harder.

And if I took a cutting here or there and rubbed it into flame
and from that warmth was the only beneficiary (typical human),
know first that it was a selfish heat, but second that smoke is a kind of
communication.

Same for the paper I sliced from the heartwood, same for the splinter
pens, whose aim
was not to confine you to words but to write you back into yourself. A poetry
that knows the tree makes all these things, but also these things make the tree.

Isla Verde II   (Green Island, or Giving)

50°75'67 S, 75°16'60 W

From me, you took what took me years to grow and made a culture.
You couldn't name me by the shape of my leaves, but you were sure,
on sight, that there was wood enough in me for a boat's-worth

and so you made one. I gave over to the process
and its Greek-strange vocabulary, and saw my own language to be at a loss.
I gave over to being worked and steam-bent, to being pitched the very
colour of the earth.

You didn't stop there. You licked your upper lip and got to work:
smaller things first, not vital things but good to have – a wine cork
so you wouldn't have to kill the bottle, charcoal, ladles, toothpicks.
Then, things that could break and later you would have to fix –
a chair you could sink into, but might not fully support your weight,
parquetry that frets from wear, a crossbeam that sags if you hang from it.
All these things you put into the boat, and the boat you put out on the water
and I thought there couldn't be wood left in me, when from the pith of me
you chipped a matchstick, lit it, saw me better.

Isla Peligrosa   (Dangerous Island, or Red Flag)

43.9842°S, 73.673°W

I am pure form.   I laugh too easily.   My
harbours are deep by nature.   I am that rare thing that snow
does not improve.   I bloom early, shed late.   Roots
 tend not to have to reach in me for anchorage.   My birds sing well, or well
enough not to be noticed.   My land doesn't slide because heights
don't bother it.   I do accede to gravity.   I cry a mite too hard.   Other
islands envy me, none emulate.   I wouldn't be myself if I were different,
 would I?   I am where the film begins, I'm the tuning fork, the entrance
hall, the overture,
the mise-en-scène.   My waters lap, my waters suck their teeth.   I am
 the mirror of cloud and the mirror of cloud-lack.   I am
rolling my eyes.   My slopes are no steeper than love-handles.
I wear all colours; all colours go with me.   I am not fully above the sea,
and therefore neither secrecy.   I am where the poem lands.

Isla de la Boca   (Island of the Mouth)

43.7995°S, 72.9634°W

Every island is a mouth in that
what we see
of the inner workings
is nothing
but the shape it eventually takes.

Unfair, then,
to tell it to speak,
then pack the chasm drawn
when breath is drawn
with quartzites and soil
and the metal used in phones
and hangover-water from the ice age
and tar and pitch and bitumen

then wonder
why you are not entertained.

Isla Ballena   (Whale Island, or The Orphan Tsunami)

52°16'92 S, 74°50'57 W

It's not that

it didn't come from
anywhere in particular. It's

that it didn't have to. What
doesn't have a name needs none:
it is itself, fully, without us. Thus

it came: nameless, fatherless, expensive. It
had no need for us, which is worse, and made
its coming all the grimmer. And really this is the meat of it –
we do not summon destruction on our heads,
whatever our psychology; it gathers itself

behind the horizon, where the seas
are hungriest, and lands. There's
a chance, of course, that it's

God, either in the doing or
in the thing. Like God, it

never ends.

Tierra del Fuego   (The land of fire, or The Passive Voice)

54°00'00"S, 70°00'00"W

I did consent to the tempest.
You don't know: it is pure touch to be spat at, come at,
picked up and thrown down; to be touched
is to be proven. A storm never takes from its arsenal
the same water twice. It makes glass of me.
At night I try to read its text
but really touch is the only thing with meaning
my broken neck; the way my skin twists; my better hand, broken.
It pants its way to sleep
and believe me, it means all this as a compliment:
victims, after all, are chosen.

Tierra del Fuego   (The land of fire, or Pearl Button)

54°00'00"S, 70°00'00"W

Every so often the sea puts a pearl between my toes
and I have to determine if it's worth keeping
or if it's just some ghost it couldn't bear to live with any longer.

Tierra del Fuego   (The land of fire, or The Infinitive)

54°00'00"S, 70°00'00"W

To be born, to bear, to be born, and so on.
To want nothing.
To sleep at all times. Not to budge.
To course through the worm and be better for it.
To sink and sink.
To sew, to rip asunder, to sew, and so on.
To catalyse life. To retard it.
Not to love or accept love.
To rebuff language. To speak anyway.
To rise or age.
To eat, to bring up, to eat, and so on.
To hold only what falls. To safekeep.
To open the mouth, and wait.
Not ever to love.
To become what becomes of you.
To go on.

Isla Golondrina   (Island of Swallows)

54.86'67°S, 70.35'00°W

And all I can do is ask that you come back;
I cannot ask you, in the first place, not to go.
But please remind me that you're not the cormorant:
that you didn't fully sink, that you were only flying low,

that the night was not unanimous –
you were inside it all this time, keeping things light.
Somehow I have faith: the hair on my neck
stood only for the wind, and not your ghost, yet.

You are not a thing of romance, like a wolf or a shipwreck, I know:
wolves and shipwrecks do not go – they keep to their lairs.
They're not like you. They don't do tricks behind the snow and then breeze
into the house again, carrying pomegranates back from God-knows where.

Islote(s) Solitario(s)   (Solitary Island(s))

54.97'03º S, 67.12'39º W
52.28'33º S, 73.61'67º W
51.67'67º S, 74.74'96º W
47.70'02º S, 75.33'61º W

The worst thing in the world is restless land.
Imagine you are land and do not want to be –
you jerk and shudder just for movement's sake
and all your animals peel off from you like dandruff.

So one day (in the future they'll say: according to legend)
you hoist up your skirts, head for the sea,
land yourself right in the midst of it.
You are a saint in hermitage, you make hosts of kelp.

But saints, of course, have their disciples.
Just one at first. Then another, and another.

Isla Decepción   (Disappointment Island, Antarctica, Claimed by Chile)

62°58'37 S, 60°39'00 W

You can't ask the universe for happiness,
which anyway mightn't even exist here in our world of things,
which is not a world of ideas of things. Ask instead for artifice,

the ersatz, the second best,
for a good bit better than nothing,
but still not quite, outright, for happiness.

Wasn't the answer like landing the kite, and the guess
like flying it? Wasn't the upcoming vaster than the coming?
This, basically, is the art of it.

Contentment with your lot is just admitting you have less
than everything:
ask for happiness

and you're asking too for freedom, beauty, brotherhood, justice,
the cod-laws of merit and deserving.
It's artifice

you want, pretence and painlessness,
the absence of asking.
The distance from that heart to this
is enough, is in excess.

Isla Olvidada   (Forgotten Island)

42.12'67°S, 72.61'38°W

Either way, they named their forgetfulness – a low blow.
Isla Olvidada, I know. I know, I know.

Isla Luz   (Island of Light)

45.48'61˚S, 73.95'31˚W

To swim is to take the place water has earned
and it won't be moved so easily – I am undeserving volume.
Between light and me is present water, water yet to come.
The only thing for it is to swim and from the swimming somehow learn.

A human in water – I am pushing rope, I am counting air.
Boats giggle into their chests at me. I am threading eyelets.
On the water the hours lengthen like strings of saliva. They are huge and quiet.
Fish are like knives. Undertow is a bunting of knives. I don't get far.

And then there's this thing about light: that it's an island,
it's a place, an event, you can swim to it, it's something you attend.
It's a word that hasn't been used yet in a lie.
It's a guest at the dinner table, not joking but smiling, reserved but not shy.
The heart that knows it never will, but thinks it might.
To find on the sea a patch that is not sea, and call it Light.

Santiago

33.4489°S, 70.6693°W

Out on the water there is a table
and at the table an empty chair.
They have bared their palms and let fall from them
the best of what they have:
some pale tomatoes,
some apples that would rather not be apples.
They've boiled a pig's head to resemble a drawing of itself –
this is the centerpiece.
Someone has placed, for you, on good porcelain,
a slice of something too sweet
because they thought you'd like it.
They have left you also a sprig of jacaranda on the side.
The wine is as dark and as bitter as hash.
The salt shifts on the waves underfoot.
There isn't much wit or irony.

Here is what you do:
you go out on the water
and you sit
and you eat.

Isla Huerta   (Allotment Island, or The Plot of Land)

43°62'08 S, 72°97'80 W

It starts, as always, midway through: out of nowhere
came a topsoil square in the corner of the garden
accented against the grass like the current month on a calendar.
The hero smirked to see his hands harden
and the mud tuck crescent moons beneath his fingernails.
Yes his heart was in it, but you cannot water seeds with blood
or stroke a carrot into fullness or threaten the runt crocus to smell.
He looked on what he had done, and it was no good:
it was a snapshot of tundra; a foetal fruit that shirks from ripening;
a row of beans like cocks at a urinal;
a door into darkness; a growth not quite requited.

Isla Nueva   (New Island, or Forecast for the Year Ahead)

46.49'45°S, 74.33'42°W

With any luck, you will pick mushrooms this autumn.
The birches will surely have kicked up enough for a bucketful,
their barcode shins, as I have imagined them, brittle as ash.
And as you amble and squat, their stately yellow heads,
rigid in the thinning sun, tilt like Jesus toward the meek.

The winter please God will pass quick. Say you take a week
on a lesser Antille – the long dark slopes on either side
won't be long steepening: you'll glide into the clock-change.
You'll share a blanket, something chequered, cashmere,
spilling wine on it, rubbing popcorn salt from your fingers.

There will be white mornings, rooms of light and silence,
small movements of hair, ejaculations of buds, late snow.
Things are slower now, still hard, but more and more familiar,
and the thought of someone else's heart inside yours is acceptable.
Touch wood it won't grow too big, or bigger than your heart, and beg for
                                                    release.

If all goes well, the skies will hold. The tarpaulins will stay drawn,
the pedalos unmoored, the country's tricycles upright. One of you
will at least halfknow the language, but still, farcically, misorder something.
All night you will quietly fuck on the balcony, the guidebook flapping
in the breeze, and the boats on the marina, agreeing with each other.

Epilogue / Islas de la Memoria

Islote Cabeza (Head Island)
53.1367°S, 72.2293°W
Smaller now, in retrospect, the shore
has shrunk to the hairline of a neck:
the smell and taste and texture of sand, more or less.

Isla Tres Dedos (1) (Three Fingers Island)
45.2909°S, 74.5729°W
the ring, which signaled me to stay.

Grupo Barba (Beard Islands)
45.3566°S, 73.7105°W
The ultimate con.
From up close: many.
From far away: one.

Islote Iris (Iris Isle)
47.2486°S, 74.3237°W
These are the colours an island can be:
green, blue, grey, brown, the colour of an orange,
universe blue, rain blue, rain
brown, home, love, folksong blue.

Isla Tres Dedos (2) (Three Fingers Island)
45.2909°S, 74.5729°W
the middle, which had nothing much to say.

Isla Foot (Foot Island)
49.3811°S, 74.3951°W
in English, somehow. I imagine someone,
with their own tears and their own hair,
washing it as you'd wash the godhead –
for your sins.

Isla Corazon (Heart Island)
        ??.????°S, ??.????°W
the subject / object of the heart.

Isla Tres Dedos (3) (Three Fingers Island)
        45.2909°S, 74.5729°W
and the index, which pointed me away.

II

Isla del Muerto   (Island of the Dead, or In Case of Death)

38°42'21 S, 73°9272 W

1. Cessation of Breath: Is He Breathing?

He's not breathing, and he cannot go on like this. He needs air. Mouth-to-mouth is a fool's game: you must not believe that you have enough air for the both of you. The body should supply itself, but in this it can be encouraged. Breath begets breath, and life life. One O says yes to another O and that equals oxygen. One god nods to the next god, who nods to the next and so on. Therefore plant plants, as follows:

(i)   The chest is just a gathering of shapes as it is, and it's not such a leap to liken it to a kind of shrubbery: there is depth and breadth enough for soil; it lends itself naturally to inhabitance, and from there to conurbation.
So drop seeds and sow. It grows in spite of itself.

(ii)   The extremities are a framework already in place: honeysuckles, for example, thrive on the order inherent in limbs; fingers are the beginnings of mathematics, and you will find the sweetpea loops nicely to a ring; ivies are many and incessant.

(iii) You must think of the holes of the head as a blessing. Eye sockets, in particular, are favourable to succulents.

2. Cardiac Arrest: Is There Any Rhythm to Him?

They say: cut the wood yourself and it will warm you twice. It is the same for the heart – if you beat it, it will beat. And it is the same with blood – it won't move unless you move it. This is the kind of work that must be done by hand. This is monks and manuscripts. This is sculpture. This is the work your father did, is where you came from.

(i)	Locate the heart by feeling
(ii)	Trace out the gridlocked veins
(iii)	Prepare the bell for pealing
(iv)	Make fists and take your aim
(v)	Pound it till it feels like kissing
(vi)	Push the blood between your hands
(vii)	Force the heart to miss what's missing
(viii)	Breathe into it what breath you can
(ix-xii)	Of all the laws that you could leave him
	leave him only one:
	hurt could your heart every man,
	hurt can his heart none.

3. Pallor Mortis: What Colour is He?

Isn't it tempting to leave him? Now that you know he's as white as you? Is there no way he could live like snow lives, which is to say: unanimously, without discrimination, everywhere, carelessly/carefully, in paralysis, absent, and dumb? No: that is the opposite of science, and you should proceed like so:

(i)   Hit him. The pocket-bursts of red that follow every blow remind the skin of its duty.

        (a)   This is not advisable for the lips, which, if blue, should be bitten, as before.

        (b)   This is also, NB, only a temporary reversal of the state.

(ii)   If saffron seems like an investment, remember that its employment requires the body to steep (and steep and steep) and be bathed. Did your hands memorise the weight of his? Well then, now's your chance: knead the yellowing water into him, notice the steady dawning of your skins. Saffron is pittance.

(iii)   Failing this, cow's piss has been known to do the trick.

(iv)   There is always war paint. Humans have been making themselves up for years. They are canny and, often, uncannily like themselves. It's a neat manoeuvre, but you, of course, would always know.

4. Hypostasis: Has His Blood Settled?

Bloodset / Blooddown: when the body designs its own horizon in telling the red blood cells: Rest now or Settle. And they do, in good faith, like children called to come down at once from the trees: with a pause, then dripping one by one from the canopy. With relief. With the sound, even, of relief, the deflation of that last f. The way a bus is grateful to be waved down, the way a coal chimney genuflects and savours its own condemnation. In such a way does the blood settle, and its acceptance is crepuscular. To cause a blood-rise you must:

(i)   Reverse gravity.
(ii)   Reverse time.

5. Algor Mortis / Decline in Temperature: Look Up: Could You Pick Him Out in a Crowd? Is He Redder, More Gigantic Than Before? Is He Whiter? Tinier? Is He Closer To / Further From Land? Is He Different, Depending on Your Location, or Constant? Is He Causing Havoc to Radio Signals? Would It Mean Sudden Death to Approach Him? Blindness to Look? Or Do Those Advances Neither Put In Nor Put Out On Him? Does He Remain Unmoved? Are You in the Sweet Spot? Is It Down to Him What Gets Eaten and What Fed? Does He Cultivate Your Farthest Points? Is He Beautiful at Your Edges? Does He Still, Albeit Rarely, Tilt Your Tired Face Towards His? Must He Always Remain This Way, Never to Swell or Contract, For You to Be Happy? Listen. Are You Satisfied or Not?

It is considered a strength to find yourself in any given room and still know where North is. In the same way, you should be able to read a dwelling, know if he is adding to it or taking away or if there would be no difference without him. Assuming the latter:

    (i)   You could melt him, but he would not flow.
    (ii)   You could torch him, but he'd burn too slow.
    (iii)   You could fuck him, but he wouldn't know.

6. Rigor Mortis: Can He Yet Be Turned?

By now it should be clear. You are on a boat deck, both of you, and a white sun fizzes on the water as though dropped like an aspirin. Then it dissolves completely. Darkness. Two unseeable faces, etched uselessly into smiles. You cast out a word or two and they frost over with brine: each stroke of the pen is breakable. Things snap or creak and you credit these sounds to him, but these are equally plausible: the sucking of a mussel; the canvas being canvas; the scissorwork of seagull wings; one sea creature tearing the flesh from another sea creature; a jellyfish pulsing past like the ghost of a heart; sounds of your own invention; your own thrown voice. You line up his armpit hair to the marram grass on the shore, and the parallax is kind: they are near enough to a perfect fit. You recount the boat parts: Forestay. Gunwale. Thwart. Tiller. Transom. Jib. Clew. Keel… Even if he was moving, he might as well be doing it behind the ocean, somewhere utterly else.

(i)   Wait.

(ii)   From the bilges of hopelessness, skim the oldest foam and the darkest pitch, and from the oldest foam and the darkest pitch, procure the lowliest gnat, the sickliest, and

(iii)   Name it thus: His Finger Twitched.

7. Decomposition: Has He Broken Down?

Once, you decided to catalogue life. It was a losing game, but even then you knew what was and wasn't reversible and therefore you persisted. You constructed his every last hair – the one that flags age; the ancient; the wisps; the cowslicked. You thought of digestion, the blanket alchemy of browning, that shyest of Chinese whispers. You thought of nerves. There were:

1. assemblies of cells;
2. parliaments of bone, bipartisan clicks, bickering, motions, stalemates, and the endless legislation of movement and stasis;
3. two sides, the right of which dictated;

When you dreamt hard, you could make a nail erupt. Dreamt lighter – the skin of a lip, a scar, the stirrup. Bigger, bolder things too, like

a. breath. The stuffy grammar of it. How it guffaws at the smallest misstep;
b. the subject/object of the heart;
c. the check and balance of breath;
d. two feet, two pliant, compliant feet, two suffering feet, two poor feet God love them;
e. all kinds of erections;
f. the idea, in his mind, of an I. Distinct from you, who to him is: Him;
g. the glacier game, the earthquake, the seaswell, the henpeck we call "breath".

You wrote blood, and then you wrote it in Greek, and then the whole thing fell into translation, into action.
Reaction: he turned.
He turned on you.
He withered in your hand, flopped out.
It was a time after Babel, when everything you had named was suddenly anonymous.
Falsehood is not in words: it is in things.
He feeds himself to the world, one parachute tooth of the dandelion by

one, their damage doing, doing, done.
You cover your mouth and nose.

(i)   compose again.

Acknowledgements

The idea for what has variously been called 'islas', 'islands', 'unnamed island project', 'islands 2', 'project title TBD', 'islands 3', 'islands final', 'islands final 2', and 'islands final actually final no seriously this time final 2' was born over five years ago, although as is often the case with these things, there's a prehistory to the history, and for that reason the first acknowledgment I would like to make is to the first island and the first islander: Uncle John, may he rest in peace, and his (later my) Achill, may it remain restless.

Others who led this horse to water: Mary O'Connor at Coláiste De La Salle; Judy Kravis at UCC; and Maura Dooley, Eva Salzman, and Francis Spufford at Goldmsiths, all of whose faith in my work was contagious, eventually. The often incredible and often incredulous support of my parents, Liam and Siobhán, and that of my siblings, Joanne, Billy, Eimear, and Mary, is also to blame or to thank for this book – they are ok with whatever it might have ended up turning into, which is what privilege is.

Not such a cheerleader, though no less an advocate, is Tom Ironmonger, my cleverest friend and closest reader, whose hope was that this was enough; it was. Nevada Street Poets (who know who they are) also saw many of these poems in their initial stages, and saw things and said things I would never have thought to see or say.

Iterations of these poems have appeared in *The White Review*, *The Stinging Fly*, and *Modern Queer Poetry*. The second part of the book, In Case of Death, was originally written to accompany the video art installation 'Clear as a Bell' by Rob Crosse in 2016, before finding its current, and I think final, meaning here.

Quiero agradacer tambien a todos los que en Chile me han ayudado en el proceso de escribir este libro, y a todos los que han facilitado mis investigaciones y la realización del libro final, incluyendo a los empleados del Instituto Geográfico Militar, de la embajada irlandesa de Chile, y a los conocidos y desconocidos que me han contado de sus tierras.

Finally I want to pay thanks to my editor Ben for many things, but mostly his soundness, which is the best quality. Mil gracias, chaltu may, agus go raibh maith agaibh go léir ó chroí.

Kümeafuy ñi feypiel fachi lifru mew müley kiñeke wapi wingkazungun üytungelu, ñamngelu am, kam tukulpawenolu am ñi kuyfike anünche üy. Pewmangele kimngetuay tati.
(Mañumfiñ Álvaro Calfucoy Gutiérrez fachi rulpazunguel mew.)

I would like to acknowledge that the names of the islands in this book are in Spanish because many of their original names in indigenous languages have been lost or never recorded. It is my hope that they will be relearned.